T R I L L I U M

A GUIDE TO THE COMMON WILDFLOWERS
OF NORTHEASTERN WISCONSIN

by MARY B. GOOD

ISBN   0-9627976-0-X

Library of Congress   90-93482

A HORTA PUBLICATION

Distributed by Jober Productions
                P.O. Box 1434
                Woodruff, Wisconsin 54568

Printed in the United States of America

Mary B. Good is the co-author of two _Time-Life Garden Guides_, "Trees" (vol. 5) and "Foliage Houseplants" (vol. 6). She has a M.S. in horticulture and a B.S. in communications and botany from the University of Wisconsin. A former vice-president of the Garden Writers of America Association, she has written thousands of articles for newspapers and magazines during her 25-year writing career.

This book is dedicated in memory of

LARRY MONTHEY

the Euell Gibbons of Wisconsin,

a big man with a big and warm heart

who knew more about Wisconsin's edible wildplants

than any man I ever knew.

ACKNOWLEDGMENTS

No man (or woman) is an island, or in this case, a peat bog, thus thanks go out to those who helped on this project: Hats off to Ron Good, for his drive and inspiration, Michele Morse of the M.M. Morse Agency for color design and color layouts, James D. Young for color photography, Linda Schroeder-Golding for illustrations, Alan Cook for editing the manuscript, Mary Jo Owen and Jack Owen for their generous technical support services, Art Director John Elling and Production Manager Debbie Westlund, Flambeau Litho, for their patience and expertise, "Lucky" Linda Thomas for proofreading, and Phyllis Blazkowski for the intro photo.

INTRODUCTION

Have you ever been chased by a bear? You should have been with me as I did the field research for this book. Two weeks in the woods outfitted in my mosquito jacket, my netted hat, my Deet facial makeup and my combat boots was not exactly the Easter parade. An accurate count of plant communities to establish credibility for this book meant encountering the funny friends of the forest on their turf.

First, there was the bear, drooling his way through a berry patch, when he spied me studying the ground flora. Feeling his territory threatened, he hunkered over to chase me away. I felt the earth move under my feet when the bear approached, as he stomped on saplings and dead brush. The sound and smell of an approaching bruin is something I'm sure you'd remember vividly. It's a rare moment. You'd be surprised how fast you can move. I thought I was Peter Pan instead of a middle - aged plant scientist!

It is well-known that the mosquito is our Wisconsin state bird, and the specimens I encountered on this botanical expedition were truly worthy of this nebulous title. They acted like they had never before seen human flesh. Without my insect - repellent impregnated bush jacket, God knows I'd have been carried off.

Would you like to hear about all the wood ticks that found their way under my cuffs and through my ring-around-the-collar? Or the pine snake that slithered up nose-to-nose?

The piece de resistance of this journey into the wild was the last night, when I was leaving the area, only to hit Bambi, who leaped off unharmed after doing $1600.00 damage to my car. The police suggested that I stay overnight at a motel, since I was badly shaken. They escorted me to a place nearby, a strange cabin on the Wolf River, where the water came up through the floor boards like a mini-geyser. In the morning I discovered that the cabin was built over a rapids, and the cabin looked seriously like it was about to be swept downstream. You know the place? I've never seen anything like it before, and probably never will.

Reflecting on my adventure, would I do it again? You bet I would!

------Mary B. Good, Sept. 1990

Phyllis Blazkowski photo

TRAILING ARBUTUS

Epigaea repens

Blooms: April

Habitat: Sandy forest and sunny openings on woodland hills; also shady woods under conifers

Also known as: Mayflower

First wildflower to bloom in the range, trailing arbutus,
with its clusters of pinkish-white blossoms, can be
spotted by following your nose to the source of the
haunting fragrance. While the leathery, evergreen
leaves measure three inches in length, flowers are a
wee 1/2 inch long, from the base of the tubular corolla
to the five-lobed margin. Dainty flowers are produced
in small clusters. An elusive, slightly-woody perennial,
trailing arbutus resists transplant attempts. It should
be allowed to grow and bloom where it is planted by
nature, not by man. The Pilgrims were said to be
particularly disposed to arbutus because the sight of
it meant they had survived the death-dealing New
England winter. A true harbinger of spring!

SPRING BEAUTY

Claytonia virginica

Blooms: April-May

Habitat: Rich, open woods

Tiny, pastel flowers and slender pedicels on
delicate stems say hello to spring. Ribbonlike leaves are much longer than wide. A
pair of leaves greet the flower stalk halfway
up the stem, just under the terminal raceme
of pink-rose, sometimes white, flowers. Deeper
pink veining of the petals gives the impression
of striping. This spring ephemeral rises from
a small tuber, buried deeply in the ground.
A Cinderella of spring if you spot it!

THE BUTTERCUP FAMILY

ROUND-LEAVED HEPATICA

Hepatica americana

Blooms: April-May

Habitat: Dry woods

Also known as: liverleaf

Hepaticus means liver in Latin, and the word refers
to the supposed resemblance of the leaf's shape to
that of the human liver. Hepatica is among the
first wildlings to bloom in spring, amid dead,
brown winter leftovers. Round-leaved hepatica is
most often found in decidedly-acid woods, while its
counterpart, Hepatica acutiloba, the sharp-lobed
hepatica, prefers more neutral or limey soil. Pastel-
tinted flowers are buttercuplike and vary in subtle
shades of pink, white, lilac and light blue. Unmis-
takable I.D: hairy stem and leaf underside, and
3-lobed, evergreen leaflet.
Pixie perfect!

SWEET COLTSFOOT

Petasites palmatus

Blooms: April-May

Habitat: Wet woods, swamps

Off-beat sweet coltsfoot blooms its scapose white heads in nearly-naked array, before the palmately-lobed leaves appear. Flower stems are short, crinkly, with scalelike bracts along the margins. Sweet coltsfoot comes out early, so you get a look at it before the mats of leaves carpet the wet ground. Sweet coltsfoot is not to be confused with coltsfoot, Tussilago farfara, which has yellow flowers and rounded or heart-shaped leaves, and is not found in northern Wisconsin.
Oddly absorbing!

BLOODROOT

Sanguinaria canadensis

Blooms: April-May

Habitat: Rich woods

Also known as: puccoon

The roots of bloodroot are poisonous, but North American Indians used the red sap for dye over centuries. Bloodroot springs from a fleshy rhizome to a height of 6-12 inches tall.   An interesting, palmately-lobed leaf is produced by the plant.   It is a pale leaf that clasps a stipe, bearing a white $1\frac{1}{2}$ inch, butter-cuplike flower which lasts for about a week. Not bad for starters in the season!

THE BUTTERCUP FAMILY

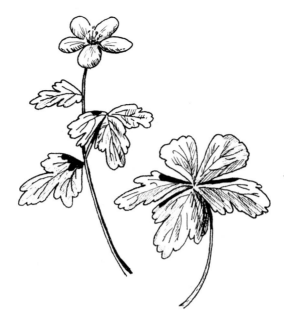

WOOD ANEMONE

Anemone quinquefolia

Blooms: April - June

Habitat: Dry to medium open woods and clearings

Smallest of the wild anemones, the wood anemone grows to only 2-8 inches tall and bears a solitary white (or faintly pinkish) flower, usually of five sepals.   The plant is slender and delicate, with three-parted, toothed leaves, often deeply cleft.

Like some other members of the Buttercup Family, such as hepatica, meadowrue, marsh marigold, and clematis, true petals are lacking in the anemones, leaving just sepals in the perianth.   A common wildflower of early spring in woods throughout the range.   A little charmer!

JACK—IN—THE—PULPIT

Arisaema triphyllum

Blooms: April-June

Habitat: Medium to wet woods

Also known as: Indian turnip, dragonroot

If you use your imagination, it seems that Jack (the 4-7 inch long flowering spadix) is preaching to a teeny audience from the arching back of the pulpitlike spathe.   The color of Jack's pulpit depends on the amount of sun or shade it gets. The spathe may be purple and white striped inside, and green, purple, or bronze on the outside.   The plant's large leaves are deeply divided into three leaflets.   Jacks grow to a height of 9-24 inches.   In summer, the spathe withers away to reveal a cluster of bright, red berries at the base of the spadix.   Although the berries have an acrid taste, Indians used to boil and grind them for use with venison.   The berries are <u>poisonous</u> if eaten raw.   Super-duper!

WINTER CRESS

Barbarea vulgaris

Blooms: April-June

Habitat: Disturbed, moist ground; fields; roadsides

Also known as: yellow rocket

Weed or wildflower? It's edible, sweet-scented, and provides a pretty yellow glow to a field abloom with it, so who's to say? A biennial that can be as small as eight inches or as tall as 32 inches, yellow rocket has 1-5 pairs of shiny, laterally-lobed leaves. The terminal lobe is larger than the others. Flowers of this wildling are 4-petaled and arranged in racemes. The fruit ..is a Mustard Family silique, or a valved pod, and winter cress' silique is 4-angled and an inch long.
At least it cuts the mustard!

THE ORCHID FAMILY

PINK MOCCASIN FLOWER

Cypripedium acaule

Blooms: April - June

Habitat: Tamarack bogs, pine woods, acid soil forests, cliffs; thrives in the company of hemlocks

Also known as: pink lady's slipper orchid

You'll find this shade-loving insect trap to be easily-recognizable in bloom by its conspicuous pink (sometimes white) inflated sac. The plant grows 6-12 inches tall and sports two large oval leaves with parallel veining surrounding each stemless flower stalk. A single, drooping, rose-lipped orchid is produced.
It usually takes from 12-15 years for the seeds of a lady's slipper to grow to flowering size. Since the lady's slipper seldom transplants successfully, it's a mortal no-no to snatch it up. A beauty to behold!

THE BUTTERCUP FAMILY

MARSH MARIGOLDS

Caltha palustris

Blooms: May

Habitat: Streambanks, roadside ditches, wet meadows

Also known as: cowslip, May-blob

The golden-yellow flowers of marsh marigolds color
the spring landscape, and mean a new batch of
pickled capers for wildfood gourmands--the tender,
unopened flower buds are relished by some people.
The hollow-stemmed plants can grow from 8 - 24
inches,   with large, kidney-shaped leaves, sometimes toothed, sometimes entire, always simple and
alternate on the stem. Golden sepals are glossy
and petallike.   Stamens are numerous. The bright
yellow blossoms are 1¼-2 inches in diameter. They
are easily spotted from the road in shallow, wet
ditches. A golden show!

THE LILY FAMILY

YELLOW DOG-TOOTHED VIOLET

Erythronium americanum

Blooms: May

Habitat: Rich moist woods in sandy, decidedly-
acid soil

Also known as: Trout lily, fawn lily, adder's tongue

This plant is stuck with an inapt nickname--it's not a
violet at all, but a lily. Dog-toothed refers to the
shape of its small, underground bulb, a detail which
further throws off most people. This low-growing
plant produces two, basal, arched leaves, with curious,
brown and whitish mottling. A solitary, nodding ,
yellow flower grows between the mottled leaves.
Blossoms measure two inches long. The flower petals
are gracefully reflexed, and each flower lasts hardly
more than a day. Tapering leaves sheathe the base
of the flower's leafless stem. Small but cute.

THE LILY FAMILY

WHITE TRILLIUM

Trillium grandiflorum

Blooms: May

Habitat: Dry to medium humusy, wooded slopes;
neutral to slightly-acid soil;
in hardwood forests

Most familiar and showiest of the early spring
wildflowers, white trillium is the subject of our
cover. Flower parts and leaves are in 3's. Large
floppy flowers measure 2-4 inches across. The
3-petaled flowers, with wavy petal margins, are
handsome, solitary, and somewhat long-lasting,
holding their beauty for two weeks or more. Aging
flowers tend to take on a pink cast. Plants vary
in height from 6-18 inches.
Trilliums will thrill 'em--a 10!

WHITE BANEBERRY

Actaea pachypoda

Blooms: May-June

Habitat: Rich, moist woods

Also known as: doll's-eyes, white cohosh and
snakeroot

A comely spring fling with large, compound leaves
on 1½-3 foot red stems. Leaflets are deeply cut,
pointed, and toothed. Tiny, white flowers are
borne on a terminal spike that is much longer than
broad. It is the black-dotted, white fruit, known
as the doll's-eyes, that grabs all the attention.
Wish there were more of this doll up North!

THE DAISY FAMILY

PUSSY-TOES

Antennaria neglecta

Blooms: May-June

Habitat: Sandy roadsides, dry fields

Also known as: ladies' tobacco

Only 3-12 inches tall, this plant might go unnoticed
if it bloomed later in the season when there are
more wildlings in bloom.   Fuzz clusters cap off
wooly stems in a creation that makes the imagination
stretch a bit to conjure up pictures of kittens' paws.
A basal rosette leaf arrangement has scalelike leaves
up the stem.   It's said that the stems of pussy-toes
were chewed by Indians, as we chew gum.
Mediocre--not exactly the cat's meow!

WILD SARSAPARILLA

Aralia nudicaulis

Blooms: May -June

Habitat: Wet woods and cool forests

Also known as: sassparilla

Curiously, the Aralia family has a great number of species that are native to the tropics. Wild sarsaparilla, however, is right at home in woodsy Wisconsin. Sometimes confused with dwarf ginseng (a cousin) or poison ivy (no relation) by the casual hiker, wild sarsaparilla has been used in the past to relieve the sting of insect bites. It grows to one foot. The plant has a single leaf, divided midway up the stem into three leaflets. Each leaflet is further divided into three or five. The foliage is often bronze when it first appears, then turns a healthy green. Several small umbels of whitish-green flowers, rounded and wispy, arise on a leafless stem, somewhat shorter than the leafstalk itself. Useful plant, unimpressive flower.

THE DOGWOOD FAMILY

BUNCHBERRY

Cornus canadensis

Blooms: May-June

Habitat: Moist, open woods

Also known as ground dogwood, dwarf cornel

A beautiful sight in spring is a cloud of white
bunchberry bracts festooning the landscape,
like the delicate palette of a Lilleputian artist.
A low-growing perennial that forms a slender,
creeping rootstock, bunchberry supports a
short, erect stem of whorled leaves. Obscure,
tiny, yellow flower clusters are enveloped by
four beautiful white bracts, which are often
mistaken for the smaller flowers. The fruit is
a cluster of bright red berries. The bunchberry is a tiny Northern cousin of the lovely
white flowering dogwood of the southern
environs. Field-finding tip: Leaves, usually
six in each whorl, are prominently parallel-
veined. A bunch of fun!

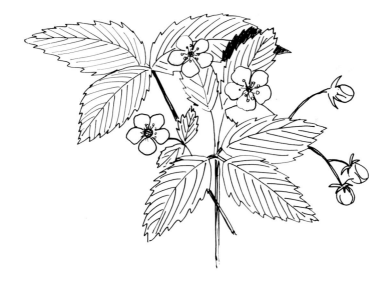

WILD STRAWBERRY

Fragaria virginiana

Blooms: May-June

Habitat: Dry sunny hills and fields, borders of
woods, moderately-acid soil

A rose is a rose is a rose, even when it's a wild
strawberry.   This member of the Rose family is
best for jam-making, delectable as a field nibble,
even though it is so small--only 3/4 inch diameter.
Plants spread by slender, horizontal runners which
sprout tufts of compound, 3-toothed leaflets.   White
flowers are clustered at the tip of a scape that is
shorter than the leaves.   The fruit of the strawberry
is not actually a berry, it is an achene--one of the
multiple hard seeds on the surface of the fleshy,
greatly-enlarged, juicy, red receptacle that gives us
that great tasting treat.   A wild delight!

THE LILY FAMILY

WILD LILY OF THE VALLEY

Maianthemum canadense

Blooms: May-June

Habitat: Cool, moist sandy woods
             in moderately-acid, humus-rich soil.

Also known as: Canada mayflower

Who knows why this plant is called wild lily of the
valley? It looks nothing like the real thing. But no
matter, it has a charm all its own --from its minute,
fragrant flowers to its zigzag stem. Wild lily forms
woodland mats of shiny, green foliage with small,
starry flowers in the month of May. Low-growing
(4-6 inches), wild lily produces just two, heart-
shaped leaves, oval and pointed at the tips with
a narrow, v-shaped sinus. Flower parts are in
4's, instead of the usual lilylike 3's.
A mat of blooming mayflowers is quite a
paintable picture!

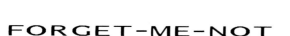

FORGET-ME-NOT

Myosotis scorpioides

Blooms: May-June

Habitat: Wet woods, swampy stream margins

A low-lying sky blue haze on the horizon may mean
you've fallen upon a patch of forget-me-nots.
Small herbs with blunt, slightly-hairy little leaves,
the enchantment of this spring wildling is its
tiny (1/4 to 1/3 inch) sky blue, 5-petaled flower
with a yellow eye.   Delicately-tinted flowers
uncoil in a spiral group.   The height of the plant
varies from 4-18 inches.
A pretty thing in a small package!

WOOD BETONY

Pedicularis canadensis

Blooms: May-June

Habitat: Dry forest and clearings; wet meadows

Also known as: fern-leaved lousewort

Wood betony rarely grows over a foot tall; its
herbage is hairy.   The leaves are fernlike, toothed,
and pinnately-lobed.   The flowers are produced on a
dense, terminal spike, interspersed with leafy bracts.
Flowers are yellow or red (or both), and sport a
beaked upper lip and a crested, 3-lobed lower lip.
There is a family resemblance in the flower of wood
betony to its cousins the snapdragon, the turtlehead,
and the skullcap.

A pleasant wildflower that gets the unpleasant name
of lousewort from an old wives' tale.   Cattle that
grazed on the plant were said to get lice---untrue,
like most old wives' tales!

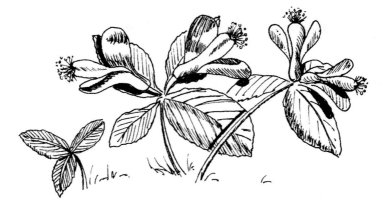

GAYWINGS

Polygala pauciflora

Blooms: May-June

Habitat: Rich woods, low ground, wet pinelands

Also known as: fringed polygala

Some people see this plant and think it is an orchid--
the rose pogonia. But gaywings is easily distinguished from rose pogonia by the whorl of upper
leaves clustered at the tip of the stem just under
the flowers. Pogonia, on the other hand, has no
such tufty whorl. Gaywing leaves are shiny and
evergreen, like wintergreen, and lower leaves are
nothing more than scales on the stem. The plant
is short, never reaching more than 5-6 inches in
height. Its flowers are lovely, and conspicuous
because they can be as large as 3/4 inch on this
tiny plant. Three true petals fuse into a tube
which culminates into a fringed crest or keel.
A diminutive delight!

THE LILY FAMILY

FALSE SOLOMON'S-SEAL

Smilacina racemosa

Blooms: May-June

Habitat: Pine barrens, wooden slopes
in acid soil

Also known as: Solomon's plume, false spikenard

What's the difference between a false Solomon's-seal
and a true Solomon's-seal?   The false has starlike
clusters of white flowers at the terminal of the
16-36 inch stem, while true Solomon's-seal, Poly-
gonatum biflorum, has bell-like, paired white
flowers that hang down from the leaf axils.   Both
are found in the Northwoods, but Smilacina
racemosa a little more frequently.   Shade-loving
false Solomon's-seal is distinguished by its long,
arching stem, bedecked with zig-zag leaves.
Fruit is a speckled berry when it first appears,
turning red upon maturity.
Graceful, almost majestic!

STARFLOWER

Trientalis borealis

Blooms: May-June

Habitat: Cool woods

This little subalpine cutie is all starry.   Two
fragile-appearing blossoms with 6-7 tiny, tapered
petals, pointed like stars at the tips, crop up
within a whorl of 5-10 shiny, pointed leaves.
There are no other leaves on the stem.   The
little white corolla is just 1/2 inch wide, and
the whole plant never gets over nine inches.
It can be as short as four inches.
A little May star!

THE LILY FAMILY

LARGE-FLOWERED BELLWORT

Uvularia grandiflora

Blooms: May-June

Habitat: Rich woods

Also known as: merrybells

The word Uvularia means hanging like a uvula.
This small, woodland lily has a drooping yellow
head that is smooth inside the flower. It is
sometimes confused with perfoliated bellwort,
Uvularia perfoliata, which feels rough inside
the flower. To make matters worse, large-
flowered bellwort is more often mistaken for
wild oats, another Uvularia, but with sessile
leaves, while bellwort's leaves clasp the stem.
The bell-shaped blossoms measure 1½-2 inches;
the smooth, oval, pointing leaves sport a
forking stem. Until the blossoms are spent,
the plant always looks like it's wilting.
Droopy; makes you want to give it a drink!

Trailing Arbutus (<u>Epigaea</u> <u>repens</u>) pg. 1

Jack-in-the-Pulpit (<u>Arisaema</u> <u>triphyllum</u>) pg. 7

Bunchberry (<u>Cornus</u> <u>canadensis</u>) pg. 16

Blue Flag (<u>Iris</u> <u>versicolor</u>) pg. 33

Orange Hawkweed (<u>Hieracium</u> <u>aurantiacum</u>) pg. 46

Black-Eyed Susan (<u>Rudbeckia</u> <u>hirta</u>) pg. 47

White Water Lily (<u>Nymphaea</u> <u>odorata</u>) pg. 56

Round-Leaved Sundew (<u>Drosera</u> <u>rotundifolia</u>) pg.60

MARSH BLUE VIOLET

Viola cucullata

Blooms: May-June

Habitat: Cool, wet woods

Wisconsin's state flower is the blue violet.
Various species of Viola proliferate in the state,
but Viola cucullata is most prevalent in the
Northwoods.   In this tiny plant, no more than
5-10 inches tall,   petals are darker toward
the throat of the flower, with the lower petals
shorter and veined.   The marsh violet has
long pedicels, which enable the dainty, spurred
flower to rise above the small, heart-shaped,
slightly-toothed leaves.
Viva la viola--it'll lift your spirits!

BARREN STRAWBERRY

Waldsteinia fragarioides

Blooms: May-June

Habitat: Woods and clearings in acid, humusy soil

When is a strawberry not a strawberry? Barren strawberry is a perky spring bloomer, with yellow instead of white flowers like true strawberry. Unlike Fragaria, barren strawberry does not have runners. Further, the 3-lobed leaflets of this low-growing plant are more blunt, less obovate, than the true strawberry. And horror of horrors, barren strawberry produces no juicy red fruit, either. At least bees like it!

THE BUTTERCUP FAMILY

WILD COLUMBINE

Aquilegia canadensis

Blooms: May-July

Habitat: Dry open woods in sandy soil and rocky bluffs

Airy grace characterizes this beautiful tap-rooted perennial, whose erect branches soar to 1-3 feet. Delicately-compound leaves with many small, rounded, and lobed leaves, divided and sub-divided into threes, form an understory to the 5-sepaled, 5- petaled flower spur. The nodding, intricate flowers are $1\frac{1}{2}$ inch long, and composed of beautiful red sepals and spurs with yellow petals. Wild columbine is typically a spring flower of the May woods, but has been known to appear as late as July.   In the past, columbine was used medicinally to treat jaundice. The five long, graceful spurs on the flower are a dead giveaway to this lazy lovely!

YELLOW BEADLILY

Clintonia borealis

Blooms: May -July

Habitat: Cool woods and wet, mixed forests

Also known as: yellow clintonia, corn lily and
bluebead lily

This short-stemmed plant emerges from a creeping
rhizome. In spring, look for 2-5 glossy-green,
oblong basal leaves, surrounding a leafless flower
stalk. Nodding, 3/4 inch long, greenish-yellow ,
bell-like flowers are borne on this stipe. A
perennial and member of the Lily family, the yellow
beadlily, typically, has its flowers in clusters of
threes and sixes. Each flower has six equal and
spreading segments. In late summer and autumn,
shiny, dark-blue berries are produced. The plant
is generally 6-16 inches tall. One of the most
abundant wildflowers in the range. Look and you'll
find it!

THE BUTTERCUP FAMILY

GOLDTHREAD

Coptis trifolia

Blooms: May-July

Habitat: Wet to medium forests and bogs; mossy woods

Goldthread gets its name from its bright yellow, underground stems. A low, evergreen perennial with slender
rootstock, the plant is only 4-6 inches tall. It bears
a single, white inflorescence composed of 5-7 sepals
and five small, clubshaped petals. The plant's leaves
are compound and basal, that is, all the leaves are
produced near the ground. The leaflets are 3-lobed,
toothed, and wedgeshaped at the base. Goldthread
leaves look similar to barren strawberry, but the
yellow, rootlike underground stem confirms it is a
Coptis. You can't miss this telltale yellow thread!

THE BUTTERCUP FAMILY

MEADOW BUTTERCUP

Ranunculus acris

Blooms: May-July

Habitat: Disturbed or wet ground, fields, roadsides

The tallest (at 2-3 feet) and most familiar of the buttercups, meadow buttercup is erect, branching, and few-leaved for its size. The butter-yellow flowers have a glossy patina that look like they have been painted with clear nail polish. Leaves are palmately-lobed, alternate and compound, while leaflets are lobed and toothed. Petals overlap and are twice as long as the sepals. The entire flower is one-inch across and showy.
Toast of the meadow!

SPATTERDOCK

Nuphar advena

Blooms: May-September

Habitat: Ponds, roadside swamps,
shallow lake water

Also known as: yellow pond lily

A poor man's water lily, spatterdock lives out
its life cycle as a floating plant in fresh water.
Fleshy, horizontal rhizomes anchor the plant
in the sand beneath the water. Glabrous, 6-12
inch long leaves are held erect in shallow water.
Yellow flowers are no more than three inches in
diameter, with five or more yellow sepals marked
in green. Numerous scalelike petals form a
fringe around the base of the flat-topped stigma;
stamens are many.
Leaves are coarse and get raggedy from wind
and boat damage. Won't win the all-American
beauty award!

WILD CALLA

Calla palustris

Blooms: June

Habitat: Bogs, cold shallow water, swamps

Also known as: water arum, water dragon

The wild calla looks like a scaled-down version of
the florist's "calla lily". Neither are really lilies, but
both belong to the Arum family of plants, though
in different genera. The wild calla grows 5-10
inches tall, with a spreading, creeping growth
habit. The underground stems (rhizomes) of this
aquatic perennial have been used in northern Europe for food, in spite of the fire-hot chemicals they
contain. (The stems were ground into flour to make
bread). The sight of a marshy pool covered with a
frosting of white wild callas in bloom is eye-catching.
The season is short, so get a good look, if only
a quick look!

BLUE FLAG

Iris versicolor

Blooms: June

Habitat: Marshes, wet roadside ditches
                 pond margins, and lakeshores

Also known as: wild iris

Similar in looks to the garden variety iris, wild
iris is smaller and has thinner stems and leaves.
Graceful and swordlike , this plant can rise to a
height of 2-3 feet. Flowers are showy, but short-
lived.   Three upward-curved blue petals (called
the standards) are smaller than the boldly-veined
3-sepaled falls, that make up the flower.   The
down-curved violet falls sport a yellow base
which melds into dark venation.   Woody rhizomes
cause intestinal upsets if eaten, and are usually
considered inedible and toxic.
Flirty mainstay of the marsh!

THE MADDER FAMILY

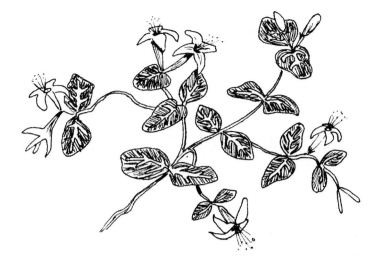

PARTRIDGE BERRY

Mitchella repens

Blooms: June-July

Habitat: Moist acid woods in humus -rich soil

Partridge berry is a ground-hugging evergreen
with paired, roundish, shiny leaves that can
creep to one foot long.   The stem roots easily at
the leaf nodes.   Leaves of the delightful partridge
berry are thin, rather than leathery, and trailing stems are slender and somewhat fragile.
Leaves measure barely 3/8 inch across.   Waxy,
white flowers, bearded within, are also produced
in pairs, at the ends of the creeping stems.   If
you miss the flowers which bloom only for a
short time in late spring, you may catch the
bright red berry that appears later and hangs
on most of the winter.   Prized in New England
partridge berry bowls.
Worth looking at, I guess, but don't kill for it!

THE BUTTERCUP FAMILY

MEADOWRUE

Thalictrum dasycarpum

Blooms: June-July

Habitat: Moist meadows and open woods

Coming upon meadowrue is like finding a cool, fringed canopy on a hot summer's day. Fringy flower clusters gently sway on the breeze. The petalless blooms with multiple stamens form a showy drooping panicle on this tall, erect plant. Rising to a height of 2-6 feet, meadowrue sports compound leaves with downy undersides and a purplish stem. The 3-lobed leaves are reminiscent of wild columbine. Tassel-like "flowers" are merely sometimes-colored stamens, since meadowrue, curiously, has no petals. The color of the stamens is variable and can be greenish-yellow, white or mauve.
Frothy and fair!

THE HEATH FAMILY

CRANBERRY

Vaccinium macrocarpon

Blooms: June -July

Habitat: Bogs and peaty swamps

Also known as: craneberry

Prostrate and creeping to three feet in length, wild cranberry waits for you on your watery adventure through the peat bog. The mat-forming plant boasts diminutive, elliptical alternate leaves on a wiry stem. The pale green little leaves are 1/4" long and slightly whitish underneath.

Small flowers are pink, recurved, and in clusters; fruit is red and no larger than 3/4" in diameter. Varieties selected for their larger berries are cultivated commercially in northern Wisconsin.
This plant is known as craneberry, because the recurved flower appears to resemble the head of a crane. A watery wonder!

COMMON MILKWEED

Asclepias syriaca

Blooms: June-August

Habitat: Roadsides, prairies, sunny fields, meadows

The coarse, rank-growing milkweed isn't much in the looks department, but it's a handy food factory to the outdoorsman .   Shoots and very young pods are a wildfood-lover's version of asparagus.   Delicious young, green, unopened flower buds taste like broccoli when boiled in 2-3 waters.   Field identification marks include 3-12 inch long, single, opposite leaves (downy on the underside) on a 3-6 foot tall stem ; milky-white, sticky juice when bruised, and golfball-sized clusters of fragrant, pinkish-mauve flowers in the leaf axils in springtime.   A close look at the semi-pendulous flower umbels will find curious, individual, hooded blossoms. Warty, gray-green pods come later, with messy, silken-haired seeds.   Follow the Monarch butterflies to this robust plant!

THE BEAN FAMILY

BIRD'S-FOOT TREFOIL

Lotus corniculatus

Blooms: June-August

Habitat: Roadsides, disturbed ground

Also known as: crow's toes, devil's claw

Why would anyone call this bright, yellow bloomer crow's toes--unless the mature fruit that hugs next year's seeds resembles the foot of a bird?   A member of the same large family of plants as that of lupine, alfalfa, clover, and vetch, trefoil is easy to nail down as a legume: the 1 inch long, narrow pod and the yellow, pealike flowers are dead giveaways. The plant, which grows to 2 feet tall, is often prostrate, but can grow erect. Trefoil sports trifoliate leaves with 2 stipules resembling leaves.   Often used for erosion control on highway banks, and sometimes used for forage, bird's-foot trefoil has naturalized on roadsides, and sandy and gravelly areas.   One for the road!

THE WINTERGREEN FAMILY

INDIAN PIPE

Monotropa uniflora

Blooms: June-August

Habitat: leaf mold; humus; in shady woods esp. coniferous woods

Also known as: corpse plant, convulsion root

One of a few waxy-white plants in Wisconsin nature. Because it is a saprophyte, absorbing its nutrients from decaying organic matter (like mushrooms do), Indian pipe is often mistaken for a fungus. Even though it doesn't make chlorophyll, it does have roots (matted roots usually attached to something partially decaying), it does reproduce by seed, and it has a stem with scalelike leaves. Indian pipe grows to 8-10 inches and has a scaly, nodding flower which becomes erect as fruit ripens. An ancient plant, Monotropa was used in folk medicine as a treatment for nervous disorders.
A fun plant, ghostly and bizarre, if you like the creeps!

SHINLEAF

Pyrola elliptica

Blooms: June-August

Habitat: Rich soil in dry woods

Our common shinleaf is large-leaved (up to 3 inches). The dull, elliptical leaves are rounded near the apex. Its flowers are spiraled, nodding, and fragrant, while the corolla is white with greenish veins. The erect flowering stalk, culminating in terminal racemes, can reach a height of 10 inches. A 4!

THE PITCHER-PLANT FAMILY

COMMON PITCHER PLANT

Sarracenia purpurea

Blooms: June-August

Habitat: Sphagnum bogs and wet, peaty woods

This carnivorous plant likes wet feet--you'll find it where the land is squishy or sopping wet. The pitcher plant catches insects, drowning them in its swollen, heavily-veined funnel. The open end of this inviting pitcher has an overarching portal, reminiscent of Jack-in-the-Pulpit. Insects are attracted by a nectar secreted around the lip of the pitcher. Just inside are downward-pointing soft spines which make exit impossible for hapless insects. They slide down into a pool of water at the bottom of the pitcher for a watery death.
A nodding, round, red flower, with umbrellalike stigmas, is produced on a separate, erect, leaf-less stem.
A botanical curiosity; leaves are more striking and remarkable than the flowers!

THE DAISY FAMILY

OXEYE DAISY

Chrysanthemum leucanthemum

Blooms: June-September

Habitat: Roadsides, sunny open fields,
              disturbed ground

Also known as: common white daisy, marguerite daisy

Naturalized from Europe, oxeye daisy carpets the
roadsides during summer with its perky, white petals.
The plant grows between 1-3 feet tall with sparingly-
branched erect stems. Leaves are irregular, narrow,
bluntly-toothed or lobed.   The white flower is 1½-2
inches across and sports a yellow center. Each stem
produces a solitary flower. The oxeye daisy looks
similar to a florist's daisy, except that the oxeye
flower is smaller and the stem is shorter and less
substantial.
A top choice of children (after dandelion) as a
snatch-up bouquet for mother!

BUTTER-AND-EGGS

<u>Linaria vulgaris</u>

Blooms: June-September

Habitat: Sandy, open woods; roadside banks;
          disturbed ground

Also known as: yellow toadflax

Some call butter-and-eggs a pervasive weed, but
look closely at this one: the flowers are grand,
golden complexities--little works of art.   An orange
egg yolk perched atop a butter-yellow lower lip
takes only a light flight of fancy to imagine.   A
narrow, drooping spur at the base of the lower lip
is also part of the floral envelope.   Flowers are
produced on clublike racemes (or spikes if you will).
Leaves are numerous, alternate, ribbonlike, and
narrowed at the base.   This perennial has been
naturalized from Europe.
A striking wild snapdragon--make mine sunny side
up!

PURPLE LOOSESTRIFE

Lythrum salicaria

Blooms: June-September

Habitat: Swamps, streambanks, shorelines

Paddling along in a canoe on a lazy, quiet northern creek, you may discover great patches of
this tall, purple spike.   A slender perennial
that looks harmless enough, the narrow, linear
leaves are paired and encircle the stem, while
flowers in the spike have 4-6 petals.
There is an organization in Wisconsin hell-bent
on eradicating this introduction from Europe
on the grounds that purple loosestrife is a
rapacious shoreline weed, usurping territory
better left for plants that support the wild-
life that find lythrum unpalatable.   In the
meantime, lythrum continues to spread and spray
its purple odium about the shorescape, exer-
cising squatter's rights.
Much-maligned, but quite a spectacle en masse!

YARROW

Achillea millefolium

Blooms: June to October

Habitat: Roadsides, fields, meadows, waste places

Also known as: milfoil, thousandleaf, bloodwort, and
                  nosebleed weed

Sometimes mistaken for a fern because of its finely
divided leaves, yarrow is an European import, as
familiar as any of our all-American weeds.   Yarrow
is a perennial that grows 1-3 feet tall.   Its stems
and branches grow stiffly erect; heads are formed
in terminal, flat-topped clusters called corymbs. Its
yellow, tubular disk flowers are surrounded by small,
whitish ray flowers.   Flowers can also be pink or
rosy-purple, as well as predominently white.   The
common names come about because the plant has as-
tringent properties and has been used in the past to
treat wounds.   The aromatic leaves are used for
making a cold-remedy tea. So-so plant.

THE DAISY FAMILY

ORANGE HAWKWEED

Hieracium aurantiacum

Blooms: June-October

Habitat: Roadsides, meadows, disturbed ground

Also known as: devil's paintbrush; also incorrectly
called Indian paintbrush in scat-
tered counties

Northerners should be familiar with this member of
the Dandelion Tribe of the Daisy Family. Orange
hawkweed is the dandelion of the North, often
confused with a relative, Hieracium florentinum,
a/k/a yellow hawkweed or king devil. Both devils
often inhabit the same turf, along with oxeye daisy.
An alien from the Old World, Hieracium picked up the
name devil's paintbrush because the colorful, coarse
wildling was considered by farmers to be a noxious
weed that ruined good pasture, and was anathema to
cattle. As an ornament on a drab roadside, however,
the sight of millions of the red-orange heads on their
hairy, erect stems is an arresting vision. No sin to
enjoy these devils!

BLACK-EYED SUSAN

Rudbeckia hirta

Blooms: June-October

Habitat: Roadsides, dry fields, waste places

Black-eyed Susan spreads a little sunshine over
the summer landscape with its yellow, daisylike
blooms.   The plant is conspicuously hairy and
rough.   It grows from 1-3 feet tall.   A short-
lived perennial, black-eyed Susan has endeared
itself as a familiar roadside ornament.   Useful
in wildflower bouquets, Susan is common and
abundant, since it tends to grow in sociable
congregations.   Yellow ray flowers number 10-15,
and are produced on a tall, slender stem.
Chocolate-colored centers offer contrast.
Good enough to be the state flower of Maryland!

PIPSISSEWA

Chimaphila umbellata

Blooms: July-August

Habitat: Dry, sandy woods, especially pine groves

Also known as: green pipsissewa, prince's pine,
waxflower

Chances are that the first time you notice this
ground-hugging evergreen herb, you'll happen
upon it by accident--when your eye is attracted
to its whorl of shiny, toothed leaves. Pipsissewa
looks fresh and bright green when most everything
else is dead. It's not often you spot this plant in
bloom, because it's so little (a mere 4-9 inches tall)
that it gets dwarfed by larger wildlings on the forest floor. The nodding flowers are white or
pinkish with a deep pink ring. The style is
conspicuously stout and conical. Pipsissewa is a
somewhat woody perennial and tends to trail and
form colonies. Choice, but not spectacular!

WILD CLEMATIS

Clematis virginiana

Blooms: July-August

Habitat: Low woods and edges of thickets, especially fencerows

Also known as: virgin's bower, old man's beard

A perennial woody vine that clambers onto other plants by clasping leafstalks, showy wild clematis prefers partial shade. It can climb 10-20 feet , and is most attractive and noticeable in fall when whitish flower panicles change into masses of silky-haired seeds--hence the name old man's beard. The vining stem produces opposite, compound leaves, each leaf composed of three oval leaflets. Western Indians chewed wild clematis leaves as a sore throat remedy. A floral gem when you can find it !

WINTERGREEN

Gaultheria procumbens

Blooms: July-August

Habitat: Open, pine woods; bog margins
in acid soil

Shiny, evergreen leaves poke up from a slender, creeping rootstock.   The leaves are leathery and elliptical in shape, while the flowers are solitary, white, waxy, eggshaped and nodding.   Petals droop from the leaf axils.   The bright, red berries are edible, having a refreshing, breath-sweetening taste.   Berries make a convenient field nibble, as they hold on through the winter, but taste best in springtime, after they've aged through the frost.   Young leaves are steeped for herbal tea.
Fragrant and well-favored by outdoorspeople!

DOWNY RATTLESNAKE PLANTAIN

Goodyera pubescens

Blooms: July-August

Habitat: Dry, acid woods in association with
             pine or oak trees

Also known as: rattlesnake orchid

Pity that such a dainty orchid should be named for
a common weed.   Its resemblance to plantain stops
with its basal rosette of oval leaves.   One of the
most striking features of this low-growing orchid
is the checkerboard leaf pattern formed by whitish
veins and cross veins on a dark background.   The
downy stem supports a 5-inch raceme of small,
white flowers, tinged with green.   In typically
orchid fashion, the tiny flower has a saclike lip.
Sepals and petals unite to form a hood over the
rest of the flower.   What a joy!

THE WATER-PLANTAIN FAMILY

ARROWHEAD

Sagittaria latifolia

Blooms: July-August

Habitat: Shallow water, pond edges, ditches

Also known as: wapato, duck potato

Bold, symmetrical lines characterize this unique aquatic plant. Distinguishing features include bright-green, arrowshaped leaf blades, and flowers in whorls of three, each flower with three large, white petals (lower ones green), on a leafless stem. Arrowhead can grow from 6-36 inches tall. It has fibrous roots and numerous runners that culminate in small tubers, $\frac{1}{2}$-$1\frac{1}{2}$ inches in diameter. These tasty, little tubers are of interest to wildfood enthusiasts. Wisconsin Indians have used the tubers as potato substitutes. With the help of a potato hook, duck potatoes are harvested in fall or spring, and boiled, baked or roasted. Just ducky!

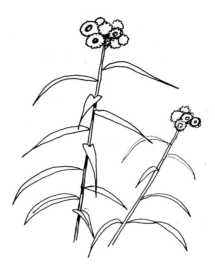

PEARLY EVERLASTING

Anaphalis margaritacea

Blooms: July-September

Habitat: Roadsides, fields, dry soil

A late summer bloomer, pearly everlasting looks something like pussytoes to the uninitiated eye, except that the stems of Anaphalis are very leafy, while pussytoes has basal leaves and only scale-like leaves along the stem.   Note, too, that pussy toes is a spring bloomer.   Both pearly and pussy are in the Aster Tribe and have white floral clusters.   Pearly's are dry, white bracts, arranged around a yellow center.   Stems grow 1-4 feet tall; leaves are ribbonlike.   Pearly's stems and leaves are white tomentose underneath, and greener above.
Anemic and uninteresting, because you're spoiled by prettier wildlings by the time July rolls around!

FIREWEED

Epilobium angustifolium

Blooms: July-September

Habitat: Wet to dry forest clearings; disturbed ground

Also known as: great willow herb

Pink spikes of fireweed are the first flowers to appear in logged-out or burned-over areas that man has raped and ruined. It is as if these orchidlike flowers form Nature's own beautification project. The long irregular racemes often form spires one foot in length on a plant that may reach a height of nearly six feet. Each floret on the spike has a slender pink calyx tube with four pink or purplish petals, totaling about an inch in length. The willowlike lanceolate leaves are simple and alternate. In autumn, long, slender seed pods split, inflate and send off airborne seeds bearing silky, homely down. Ragged-looking as the season wears on; not so hot!

JEWELWEED

Impatiens capensis

Blooms: July-September

Habitat: Shady, damp thickets streambanks;
low, roadside ditches

Also known as: spotted touch-me-not

Most species of this small family of flora grow
naturally in Africa and tropical Asia; only two
are natives of eastern USA. Of these, orange
jewelweed grows in northern Wisconsin. Jewelweed has a unique trigger seed-release mechanism
that causes fruit to explode on contact--thus the
nickname touch-me-not. The succulent, alternate
leaves and hollow, weak stems are often crushed
and rubbed on the skin as an antidote to poison
ivy, which often grows nearby. Red-spotted,
orange flowers that resemble a court jester's hat,
are pendent and conspicuous with their jaunty
spurs. An intriguing, snappy number!

WHITE WATER LILY

Nymphaea odorata

Blooms: July-September

Habitat: Ponds, shallow lake water

A mood of dreamy serenity accompanies the sight of a water lily pad, occupied by a small frog taking in summer's sun. The floating leaves are thick, entire, and platterlike. Undersides of the leaves are purplish, as are the long, ropelike stems of this plant. Showy, fragrant white flowers that remind one of cactus-flowered dahlias, gracefully tapering to a point, measure about five inches across. A morning flower, each blossom of the white water lily opens in the forenoon for three days before it is spent. An elegant ornament on the water!

EVENING PRIMROSE

Oenothera biennis

Blooms: July-September

Habitat: Disturbed ground, roadsides, waste places

The name of this plant is prettier than the plant itself.   A rank grower that can shoot up from 1-4 feet,
evening primrose is a biennial, and a good thing too,
because after it finishes its 2-season life cycle, we
can, hopefully, be done with it--unless it is a good
year for seed production.
The yellow sun-loving spicate florets are unexciting;
turn to old gold with age.   This evening-flowering
suncup has a floral section that stretches out like a
long neck.   Roots are edible as cooked vegetables
and the flat, lanceolate leaves are used in salads.
Moths love them.
Vastly over-rated!

THE DAISY FAMILY

LARGE-LEAVED ASTER

Aster macrophyllus

Blooms: July-October

Habitat: Dry or moist woods; clearings

Say hello to late summer when you see large-leaved aster bear its harvest of pale blue or violet flowers. One-half inch heads are grouped in dense, flat-topped terminal clusters. Leaves are broadly heartshaped, with a basal notch, often rough on the upperside of the leaf, hairy below. Stems are angled, stout, and reach a height of 1-4 feet. Flowering branches are sticky. Aster was used in herbal medicine in days of yore--but not now. More of a commoner, than royalty!

COMMON TANSY

Tanacetum vulgare

Blooms: July-October

Habitat: Fields, waste ground, roadsides

Robust and aromatic, the 1-3 foot tansy plant
attracts notice. Its ferny foliage and large,
flat-topped clusters of golden, buttonlike
disk flowers make a late summer show for
roadside lookers. Tansy comes to us via
Europe, where the perennial is cultivated in
grandmothers' gardens. An old-fashioned
plant with old-fashioned charm, tansy is
sometimes used medicinally as herbal tea.
Often considered a subgenus of Chrysan-
themum, Tanacetum really belongs to the
Anthemis Tribe.
Brighteyed and bushytailed!

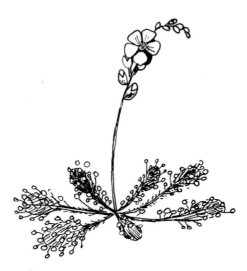

ROUND — LEAVED SUNDEW

Drosera rotundifolia

Blooms: August

Habitat: Open-water bogs; peaty, moist, acid,
and sterile marshes; inhospitable human
habitats

Peculiar insect-eating plants, bronzy sundews sport
a ground-hugging cluster of round-ended tentacles
tipped with viscid globs. In the sun, leaves appear
to glisten due to the many red-stalked hairs, giving
the leaves the appearance of having been kissed by
dew. Insects find them the kiss of death, for
attractive though they may be, the sticky hairs en-
trap the insects that venture near, and the plant
digests them.

Not terribly numerous, and not too exciting as
insect-eating plants go--sundew doesn't snap or
funnel; it just lazily catches--like flypaper.

FURTHER READING

Bailey, Liberty Hyde and staff. Bailey Hortorium·
Cornell University. 1976. Hortus Third. Mac
millan Publishing Co. New York.
Courtenay, Booth and James H. Zimmerman. 1972.
Wildflowers and Weeds. Van Nostrand Reinhold.NY.
Curtis, John T. 1971. The Vegetation of Wisconsin.
University of Wisconsin Press. Madison.
Crockett, Lawrence J. 1977. Wildly Successful Plants.
Macmillan. NY.
Edsall, Marian S. 1985. Roadside Plants and Flowers.
University of Wisconsin Press. Madison·
Fassett, Norman C. 1976.(4th printing). Spring
Flora of Wisconsin. University of Wisconsin
Press. Madison.
Ferguson, Mary and Richard Saunders. 1976.
Wildflowers. Van Nostrand. Toronto·
Hylander, Clarence J. 1968. (3rd printing).
The Macmillan Wildflower Book· Macmillan. NY.
Monthey, L. G. 1976. Foraging for Wild Food.
University of Wisconsin Extension Service. Madison.
Peterson, Roger Tory and Margaret McKenny. 1968.
A Field Guide to Wildflowers. Houghton-Mifflin·
Boston.
Rickett, Harold William. 1963. The New Field Book of
American Wildflowers. G. Putnam's Sons. NY.
Scully, Virginia, 1971 (3rd printing).A Treasury of
American Indian Herbs. Crown Publishers. NY.
Venning, Frank D. 1984. A Guide to Field Identi-
fication, Wildflowers of North America. Golden
Press. NY.
Wherry, Edgar T. 1948. Wild Flower Guide, North-
eastern and Midland United States. Doubleday. NY.

GLOSSARY

Achene
a small, dry, hard, one-seeded fruit, which doesn't open at maturity.

Alternate
(as in alternate leaves) placed singly at different heights and on different sides of the stem.

Axil
the angle between the upper side of a leaf or stem and its supporting stem or branch

Biennial
living two years only; producing foliage the first year, flowering the second

Bract
a specialized leaf or leaflike part; a foliar organ

Calyx
the outermost group of floral parts; the sepals taken as a whole, usually green, sometimes colored or petallike

Corolla
the petals taken collectively

Corymb
a short, broad, more or less flat-topped flower cluster, the outer flowers opening first

Disk Flower
one of the tubular flowers in the central part of the head (in a Composite Family flower, like a daisy), as distinguished from a ray flower

Elliptical
more or less footballshaped

Falls
the downward-curving petals on an iris

Genera
plural of Genus. A botanic classification for the usual subdivisions of Family

Lanceolate
much longer than wide; shaped like a lance, tapering toward the tip of a leaf

Lobed
having divisions extending less than halfway to the middle of the base

Neutral Soil exhibiting neither acid nor alkaline qualities

Obovate broader above rather than below the middle

Opposite (as in opposite leaves) two at a node, one on each facing side of a stem

Palmate radiating fanwise from a common basal point of attachment; shaped like an open palm (refers to leaf venation)

Parallel extending in the same direction, equidistant at all points, and never converging or diverging (refers to leaf venation)

Perennial living several years

Perianth a collective term for the floral envelopes, the corolla and calyx considered together or either of them if the other is lacking

Raceme an unbranched, elongated arrangement of flowers on a stem with pedicelled flowers

Rhizome underground stem, usually horizontal, usually emitting roots from the lower side and leafy stems from the upper

Saprophyte a plant (usually lacking in chlorophyll) living on dead organic matter

Scape a leafless flower stalk arising directly from the ground or a very short stem

Sepal one of the individual leaves of the calyx

Sessile without a stalk

Silique the long, two-valved seed pod of the Mustard Family

Sinus a recess in a margin between two lobes

Spadix	a thick or fleshy flower spike of certain plants in the Arum family, usually subtended by a spathe
Spathe	a bract or leaf surrounding a spadix
Spike	an unbranched, elongated arrangement of flowers that are sessile
Spur	a tubular projection from a flower, usually containing a nectar-secreting gland
Stamen	the male or pollen-bearing organ of a seed plant, consisting of anther and filament
Standards	the upward-curving petals on an iris
Stigma	the terminal part of a pistil, adapted for receiving pollen
Stipe	the stalk of a structure or organ when axile in origin
Tomentose	woolly
Tuber	a short, fleshy storage organ, often used for propagation
Whorl	a circle of three or more leaves